# smoothies

# smoothies

This edition published in 2009

Love Food ® is an imprint of Parragon Books Ltd

Parragon
Queen Street House
4 Queen Street
Bath BA1 1HE, UK

Copyright © Parragon Books Ltd 2007

Love Food ® and the accompanying heart device is a trade mark of Parragon Books Ltd.

Cover design by Talking Design
Photography by Günter Beer
Home economy by Stevan Paul

ISBN 978-1-4075-6969-7

Printed in China

**Notes for the reader**
• This book uses both metric and imperial measurements. Follow the same units of
measurement throughout; do not mix metric and imperial. All spoon measurements
are level: teaspoons are assumed to be 5 ml, and tablespoons are assumed to be
15 ml. Unless otherwise stated, milk is assumed to be full fat, eggs and individual
vegetables are medium, and pepper is freshly ground black pepper.
• The times given are an approximate guide only. Preparation times differ according
to the techniques used by different people and the cooking times may also vary from
those given. Optional ingredients, variations or serving suggestions have not been
included in the calculations.
• Recipes using raw or very lightly cooked eggs should be avoided by infants, the
elderly, pregnant women, convalescents and anyone suffering from an illness.
Pregnant and breastfeeding women are advised to avoid eating peanuts and peanut
products. Sufferers from nut allergies should be aware that some of the ready-made
ingredients used in the recipes in this book may contain nuts. Always check the
packaging before use.

# Contents

Just because we know what is good for us doesn't mean that we always do what is right. For example, we all know that nutritionists recommend five portions of fruit and vegetables a day and most people recognize that it is important to start the day with breakfast. However, life is lived in the fast lane these days and it is difficult to fit in shopping and cooking with the demands of work and family life.

Smoothies can make a considerable contribution to resolving this dilemma. They can be made in minutes, so saving precious time in the kitchen. They are full of nutrients and count towards the recommended 'five a day'. Many are positive powerhouses and provide a real energy boost first thing in the morning or at any time when you feel that you are running out of steam. This book is a great place to start your smoothie love affair, and the 40 fabulous recipes for stunning

smoothies will get your taste buds tingling!

Most of the equipment required for making smoothies will already exist in any reasonably well-stocked kitchen. No specialist expensive tools are required, although you might like to choose some that speed things up or make life a little easier. Blenders, food processors or liquidizers will make smoothies in seconds, so it is well worth investing in one of these if they are not part of your kitchen already. A range of cook's knives will cut through the preparation in no time, and a separate chopping board kept exclusively for fruit and vegetable preparation is essential.

The benefits of making smoothies part of your life are endless. They contain no artificial flavours, colours or preservatives, some of which are known to have adverse effects on people with allergies and on children. By preparing your own smoothies, you know exactly what

ingredients have been used, so there are no unpleasant surprises or hidden quantities of saturated fats or sugar. They offer a tasty and interesting alternative to commercial products, cost less, are usually healthier and can be adapted to your personal taste. The natural sweetness of fruit means that fruit smoothies are an easy way to reduce sugar intake without compromising on taste. And when you have a few pieces of fruit left in your fruit bowl at the end of the week, why not use them up in a smoothie – providing they are still in good condition. With so many delicious combinations to choose from, there will always be something different for you to try.

The recipes in this book have been chosen because the ingredients complement each other perfectly, creating mouthwatering, delicious smoothies. Turn to the chapter entitled 'Berry Brighteners' when raspberries and strawberries among others are in season. Kids in particular will adore the Banana & Strawberry Smoothie, a classic that will never go out of fashion. When you are feeling more adventurous, turn to 'Totally Tropical' – and try the Papaya Sweet & Sour Smoothie for something very special. 'Fresh Flavours' looks to orchard fruits such as apples and plums for inspiration, resulting in cool creations such as Perfect Plum Shake. 'Cool & Creamy' is for those indulgent days when only creamy, smooth concoctions will do. The Coffee Banana Cooler is sure to become a firm favourite! But there is no reason why you can't experiment with your own ideas – you are limited only by your imagination. Try experimenting with vegetables and create a nutrition-packed vegetable smoothie – a great way to get those essential vegetable nutrients into kids or teenagers. Take advantage of the seasonal fruit and vegetables on offer, and make smoothies part of your diet all year round.

Bursting with flavour, crammed with goodness, made in minutes and inexpensive – it is no wonder that smoothies are so fashionable.

# Berry Brighteners

*serves* 2
175 g/6 oz blueberries
150 ml/5 fl oz cranberry juice
150 ml/5 fl oz natural yogurt
honey, to taste (optional)

# berry smoothie

Put the blueberries and cranberry juice into a blender and blend for 1–2 minutes, until smooth.

Add the natural yogurt and blend briefly to combine. Taste and add honey, if you like. Blend briefly again until thoroughly combined.

Pour into chilled glasses and serve.

*serves* 2

55 g/2 oz raspberries

55 g/2 oz strawberries, hulled

225 ml/8 fl oz crème fraîche

225 ml/8 fl oz milk

1 tsp almond essence
(optional)

2–3 tbsp clear honey, to taste

# raspberry & strawberry smoothie

Press the raspberries through a nylon sieve into a bowl using the back of a spoon. Discard the seeds in the sieve.

Put the raspberry purée, strawberries, crème fraîche, milk and almond essence (if using) into a blender and blend until smooth and combined.

Pour the smoothie into chilled glasses, stir in honey to taste and serve.

*serves* 2

100 ml/3$^1$/$_2$ fl oz Greek yogurt

100 ml/3$^1$/$_2$ fl oz water

125 g/4$^1$/$_2$ oz frozen blueberries, plus extra to decorate

# blueberry thrill

Put the yogurt, water and blueberries into a blender and blend until smooth.

Pour into glasses and top with whole frozen blueberries.

*serves 2*

100 g/3$^{1/2}$ oz frozen
blackcurrants

4 scoops of blackcurrant
sorbet

100 ml/3$^{1/2}$ fl oz crème
fraîche

2 tbsp blackcurrant cordial,
plus extra for drizzling

1 tbsp water

sugar, to taste

*to decorate*

a few mint leaves

whole blackberries

# blackcurrant bracer

Put the blackcurrants, sorbet, crème fraîche, cordial and water
into a blender and blend until smooth. Taste and sweeten with a
little sugar if necessary.

Pour into glasses. Drizzle over some cordial, decorate with the
mint leaves and blackberries and serve.

*serves 2*

1 banana, sliced

85 g/3 oz fresh strawberries, hulled

150 g/5$^1$/$_2$ oz low-fat natural yogurt

# banana & strawberry smoothie

Put the banana, strawberries and yogurt into a blender and blend for a few seconds until smooth.

Pour into glasses and serve immediately.

*serves 2*

4 tbsp orange juice

1 tbsp lime juice

100 ml/3$^1$/$_2$ fl oz sparkling water

350 g/12 oz frozen summer fruits (such as blueberries, raspberries, blackberries and strawberries)

4 ice cubes

# summer fruit slush

Pour the orange juice, lime juice and sparkling water into a blender and blend gently until combined.

Add the summer fruits and ice cubes and blend until a slushy consistency has been reached.

Pour the mixture into glasses and serve.

*serves* 2

125 g/4¹/₂ oz blackberries

125 g/4¹/₂ oz blueberries

100 ml/3¹/₂ fl oz ice-cold water

150 ml/5 fl oz natural yogurt

# black & blue

Put the blackberries, blueberries, water and yogurt into a blender and blend until smooth.

Pour into glasses and serve.

*serves* 4
350 g/12 oz cranberries,
thawed if frozen

425 ml/15 fl oz cranberry
juice, chilled

300 ml/10 fl oz natural yogurt

2–3 tbsp clear honey

# cool cranberries

Place the berries and juice in a blender and blend until smooth.
Add the yogurt and the honey and blend again until combined.
Taste and add more honey if necessary.

Pour into chilled glasses and serve.

*serves* 2

2 large ripe peaches

100 g/3¹/₂ oz redcurrants

200 ml/7 fl oz ice-cold water

1–2 tbsp clear honey

# peach & redcurrant sunset

Halve the peaches and discard the stones. Roughly chop and put into a blender.

Keep 2 stems of redcurrants whole for decoration and strip the rest off their stalks into the blender. Add the water and honey and blend until smooth.

Pour into glasses and decorate with the remaining redcurrant sprigs.

*serves 2*

75 g/2³/₄ oz frozen
raspberries

300 ml/10 fl oz sparkling
mineral water

2 scoops of blackcurrant
sorbet

# raspberry &
# blackcurrant slush

Put the raspberries and water into a blender and blend until smooth.

Add the sorbet and blend briefly until combined with the raspberry mixture.

Pour into glasses and serve.

# Totally Tropical

*serves 4*

handful of cracked ice

2 bananas

225 ml/8 fl oz pineapple juice, chilled

125 ml/4 fl oz lime juice

slices of pineapple, to decorate

# perky pineapple

Put the cracked ice into a blender. Peel the bananas and slice directly into the blender. Add the pineapple and lime juice and blend until smooth.

Pour into chilled glasses, decorate with slices of pineapple and serve.

*serves* 2

2 ripe bananas

200 ml/7 fl oz low-fat natural yogurt

125 ml/4 fl oz skimmed milk

1/2 tsp vanilla essence

# banana breakfast shake

Put the bananas, yogurt, milk and vanilla essence into a blender and blend until smooth.

Serve immediately.

*serves 2*

1 ripe papaya

1/2 fresh pineapple, peeled and chopped, plus extra to decorate

150 ml/5 fl oz soya milk

300 ml/10 fl oz soya yogurt

# tropical smoothie

Peel the ripe papaya, discarding any seeds. Cut into chunks.

Place all the ingredients in a blender and blend until smooth.

Pour into glasses, decorate with chopped pineapple and serve.

*serves* 2

250 g/8 oz ripe soft papaya

200 ml/7 fl oz ice-cold water

juice of 1 lime

slices of papaya, to decorate

# papaya sweet & sour smoothie

Peel the ripe papaya, discarding any seeds. Cut into chunks.

Put the papaya chunks into a blender with the water and lime juice and blend until smooth.

Pour into glasses and decorate with slices of papaya.

*serves* 3

125 g/4¹/2 oz whole blanched
almonds

600 ml/1 pint dairy-free milk

2 ripe bananas, halved

1 tsp natural vanilla extract

ground cinnamon,
for sprinkling

# almond & banana smoothie

Put the almonds into a blender and blend until very finely chopped. Add the milk, bananas and vanilla extract and blend until smooth and creamy.

Pour into glasses and sprinkle with cinnamon.

*serves* 2

250 ml/9 fl oz natural yogurt

100 g/3¹/₂ oz galia melon, cut into chunks

100 g/3¹/₂ oz cantaloupe melon, cut into chunks

100 g/3¹/₂ oz watermelon, cut into chunks

6 ice cubes

wedges of melon, to decorate

# melon refresher

Pour the yogurt into a blender. Add the galia melon chunks and blend until smooth.

Add the cantaloupe and watermelon chunks along with the ice cubes and process until smooth.

Pour the mixture into glasses and decorate with wedges of melon.

Serve immediately.

*serves* 2

1 wedge of watermelon,
weighing about 350 g/12 oz

ice cubes

slices of watermelon,
to decorate

# watermelon whizz

Cut the rind off the watermelon. Chop the watermelon into chunks, discarding any seeds.

Put the watermelon chunks into a blender and blend until smooth.

Place the ice cubes in the glasses. Pour the watermelon mixture over the ice and serve decorated with slices of watermelon.

*serves 2*

400 g/14 oz canned guavas,
drained

250 ml/9 fl oz ice-cold milk

# guava goodness

Place the guavas in a blender and pour in the milk. Blend until well combined.

Strain into glasses to remove the hard seeds. Serve.

*serves 2*

100 ml/3$^1$/$_2$ fl oz pineapple juice

4 tbsp orange juice

125 g/4$^1$/$_2$ oz galia melon, cut into chunks

140 g/5 oz frozen pineapple chunks

4 ice cubes

slices of orange, to decorate

# melon & pineapple crush

Pour the pineapple juice and orange juice into a blender and blend gently until combined.

Add the melon, pineapple chunks and ice cubes and blend until a slushy consistency has been reached.

Pour the mixture into glasses and decorate with slices of orange. Serve immediately.

*serves* 4

1 watermelon, halved

6 tbsp fresh ruby grapefruit juice

6 tbsp fresh orange juice

dash of lime juice

slices of watermelon, to decorate

# watermelon sunset

Deseed the melon if you are unable to find a seedless one. Scoop the flesh into a blender and add the grapefruit juice, orange juice and lime juice.

Blend until smooth, pour into chilled glasses, decorate with slices of watermelon and serve.

# Fresh Flavours

*serves* 2

2 ripe apples, peeled and
roughly chopped

55 g/2 oz strawberries, hulled

juice of 4 oranges

sugar, to taste

slices of apple, to decorate

# apple cooler

Put the apples, strawberries and orange juice into a blender and
blend until smooth.

Taste and sweeten with sugar if necessary.

Decorate with slices of apple and serve immediately.

*serves 2*

1 ripe pear, peeled and quartered

1 apple, peeled and quartered

2 large red or dark plums, halved and stoned

4 ripe damsons, halved and stoned

200 ml/7 fl oz water

slices of apple or pear, to decorate

# orchard fruit smoothie

Put the pear, apple, plums, damsons and water into a small saucepan. Cover tightly, set over a medium heat and bring slowly to the boil. Take off the heat and allow to cool. Chill.

Put the fruit and cooking liquid into a blender and blend until smooth.

Pour into glasses, decorate with slices of apple or pear and serve.

*serves 2*

2 large ripe Conference pears

125 g/4$^1$/$_2$ oz frozen raspberries

200 ml/7 fl oz ice-cold water

honey, to taste

raspberries, to decorate

# pear & raspberry delight

Peel and quarter the pears, removing the cores. Put into a blender with the raspberries and water and blend until smooth.

Taste and sweeten with honey if the raspberries are a little sharp.

Pour into glasses and decorate with raspberries. Serve.

*serves* 2

1 green tea with Oriental
spice tea bag

300 ml/10 fl oz boiling water

1 tbsp sugar

125 g/4$^1$/$_2$ oz ripe yellow
plums, halved and stoned

# green tea & yellow plum smoothie

Put the tea bag in a teapot or jug and pour over the boiling water. Leave to infuse for 7 minutes. Remove and discard the tea bag. Allow to cool, then chill.

Pour the chilled tea into a blender. Add the sugar and plums and blend until smooth.

Serve immediately.

*serves 2*

250 g/9 oz ripe damsons

200 ml/7 fl oz water

1 tbsp golden granulated sugar

4 scoops of frozen yogurt (plain) or ice cream

*to decorate*

2 Italian almond or pistachio biscotti, crumbled

plums, cut in half or quartered

# perfect plum shake

Put the damsons, water and sugar into a small saucepan. Cover tightly and simmer for about 15 minutes, until the damsons have split and are very soft. Allow to cool.

Strain off the liquid into a blender and add the frozen yogurt or ice cream. Blend until smooth and frothy.

Pour into glasses and decorate the rims with the plums. Sprinkle with the crumbled biscotti and serve.

*serves 2*

8 ice cubes, crushed

2 tbsp cherry syrup

500 ml/18 fl oz sparkling
water

maraschino cherries,
to decorate

# cherry kiss

Divide the crushed ice between two glasses and pour over the
cherry syrup.

Top up each glass with sparkling water. Decorate with
maraschino cherries and serve.

*serves 2*

4 small firm pears

2 heads of elderflowers,
freshly picked (or a dash of
cordial)

1 strip of lemon zest

1 tbsp soft brown sugar

4 tbsp water

200 ml/7 fl oz semi-skimmed
milk

langues de chat biscuits,
to serve

# elderflower & pear smoothie

Peel and quarter the pears, discarding the cores. Place in a saucepan with the elderflowers, a strip of lemon zest, the sugar and water. Cover tightly and simmer until the pears are very soft. Allow to cool.

Discard the elderflowers and lemon zest. Put the pears, cooking liquid and milk into a blender and blend until smooth.

Serve immediately with langues de chat biscuits.

serves 2

1 eating apple, peeled, cored and diced

115 g/4 oz celery, chopped

600 ml/1 pint milk

pinch of sugar (optional)

salt (optional)

strips of celery, to decorate

# apple & celery revitalizer

Put the apple, celery and milk in a blender and blend until thoroughly combined.

Stir in a pinch of sugar and some salt if you like.

Pour into chilled glasses, decorate with strips of celery and serve.

*serves 2*

250 g/9 oz bottled morello cherries

150 ml/5 fl oz Greek yogurt

sugar, to taste

cherries, to decorate

# cherry sour

Put the cherries with their bottling liquid into a blender with the yogurt and blend until smooth.

Taste and sweeten with sugar if necessary.

Pour into glasses, decorate with cherries and serve.

*serves 2*

4 medium ripe plums, stoned

200 ml/7 fl oz ice-cold milk

2 scoops of luxury vanilla ice cream

# plum fluff

Put the plums, milk and ice cream into a blender and blend until smooth and frothy.

Pour into glasses and serve immediately.

# Cool & Creamy

*serves 2*

450 g/1 lb strawberries

125 ml/4 fl oz coconut cream

600 ml/1 pint pineapple juice, chilled

# strawberry colada

Place all the ingredients in a blender and blend until smooth. Pour into chilled glasses and serve.

*serves* 2

150 ml/5 fl oz milk

2 tbsp chocolate syrup

400 g/14 oz chocolate ice cream

grated chocolate, to decorate

# chocolate milkshake

Pour the milk and chocolate syrup into a blender and blend gently until combined.

Add the chocolate ice cream and blend until smooth. Pour the mixture into tall glasses and scatter the grated chocolate over the shakes.

Serve immediately.

*serves 2*

300 ml/10 fl oz milk

1/2 tsp mixed spice, plus extra to decorate

150 g/5 1/2 oz banana ice cream

2 bananas, sliced and frozen

# spiced banana milkshake

Pour the milk into a blender and add the mixed spice. Add half of the banana ice cream and blend gently until combined, then add the remaining ice cream and blend.

When the mixture is well combined, add the bananas and process until smooth.

Pour the mixture into glasses, add a pinch of mixed spice to decorate and serve.

*serves* 2

250 ml/9 fl oz milk

50 ml/2 fl oz coconut milk

150 g/5 1/2 oz vanilla ice cream

2 bananas, sliced and frozen

200 g/7 oz canned pineapple chunks, drained

1 papaya, deseeded and diced

grated coconut, to decorate

# tropical storm

Pour the milk and coconut milk into a blender and blend gently until combined. Add half of the ice cream and blend gently, then add the remaining ice cream and blend until smooth.

Add the bananas and blend well, then add the pineapple chunks and papaya and blend until smooth.

Pour the mixture into tall glasses and scatter the grated coconut over the top and serve.

*serves 2*

150 g/5$^1$/$_2$ oz frozen strawberries

100 ml/3$^1$/$_2$ fl oz single cream

200 ml/7 fl oz cold milk

1 tbsp caster sugar

mint leaves, to decorate

# strawberries & cream milkshake

Put the strawberries, cream, milk and caster sugar into a blender and blend until smooth.

Pour into glasses and serve decorated with mint leaves.

*serves* 2

100 ml/3½ fl oz milk

125 ml/4 fl oz peach yogurt

100 ml/3½ fl oz orange juice

225 g/8 oz canned peach slices, drained

6 ice cubes

strips of orange peel, to decorate

# peach & orange milkshake

Pour the milk, yogurt and orange juice into a blender and blend gently until combined.

Add the peach slices and ice cubes and blend until smooth. Pour the mixture into glasses and decorate with strips of orange peel.

*serves 2*

300 ml/10 fl oz milk

4 tbsp instant coffee powder

150 g/5 1/2 oz vanilla ice cream

2 bananas, sliced and frozen

# coffee banana cooler

Pour the milk into a blender, add the coffee powder and blend gently until combined. Add half of the vanilla ice cream and blend gently, then add the remaining ice cream and blend until well combined.

When the mixture is thoroughly blended, add the bananas and process until smooth.

Pour the mixture into glasses and serve.

*serves* 2

150 g/5$^1$/2 oz black cherries

3 large scoops of luxury
white chocolate ice cream

150 ml/5 fl oz milk

# black & white smoothie

Halve and stone the black cherries. Put these into a blender and
blend until puréed.

Add the ice cream and milk and blend briefly to mix well.

Pour into glasses and serve.

*serves* 2

350 ml/12 fl oz pineapple juice

90 ml/3¼ fl oz coconut milk

150 g/5½ oz vanilla ice cream

140 g/5 oz frozen pineapple chunks

grated fresh coconut, to decorate

2 scooped-out coconut shells, to serve (optional)

# coconut cream

Pour the pineapple juice and coconut milk into a blender. Add the ice cream and blend until smooth.

Add the pineapple chunks and blend until smooth.

Pour the mixture into scooped-out coconut shells, or tall glasses, and decorate with grated fresh coconut.

Serve.

serves 2
200 ml/7 fl oz milk
50 ml/2 fl oz single cream
1 tbsp brown sugar
2 tbsp cocoa powder
1 tbsp coffee syrup or instant coffee powder
6 ice cubes

to decorate
whipped cream
grated chocolate

# mocha cream

Put the milk, cream and sugar into a blender and blend gently until combined.

Add the cocoa powder and coffee syrup or powder and blend well, then add the ice cubes and blend until smooth.

Pour the mixture into glasses. Top with whipped cream, scatter the grated chocolate over the drinks and serve.